# Let's Explore Haiti

by Elle Parkes

BUMBA BOOKS™

LERNER PUBLICATIONS ◆ MINNEAPOLIS

**Note to Educators:**

Throughout this book, you'll find critical thinking questions. These can be used to engage young readers in thinking critically about the topic and in using the text and photos to do so.

Lerner Publications Company
A division of Lerner Publishing Group, Inc.
241 First Avenue North
Minneapolis, MN 55401 USA

For reading levels and more information, look up this title at www.lernerbooks.com.

**Library of Congress Cataloging-in-Publication Data**

Names: Parkes, Elle, author.
Title: Let's explore Haiti / by Elle Parkes.
Description: Minneapolis : Lerner Publications, [2017] | Series: Bumba books. Let's explore countries | Includes bibliographical
    references and index. | Audience: Grades K–3.
Identifiers: LCCN 2016039579 (print) | LCCN 2016040113 (ebook) | ISBN 9781512433654 (library binding : alk. paper) | ISBN
    9781512455595 (pbk. : alk. paper) | ISBN 9781512450415 (eb pdf)
Subjects:  LCSH: Haiti—Juvenile literature.
Classification: LCC F1915.2 .P37 2016 (print) | LCC F1915.2 (ebook) | DDC 972.94—dc23

LC record available at https://lccn.loc.gov/2016039579

Manufactured in the United States of America
1 – CG – 7/15/17

Expand learning beyond the printed book. Download free, complementary educational resources for this book from our website, www.lerneresource.com.

# Table of
# Contents

# A Visit to Haiti

Haiti is a small country.

It is an island.

It is in the Caribbean Sea.

Haiti has tall mountains.

It has flat plains.

It has rocky beaches.

There are coral reefs near

the shore.

Haiti has many different kinds

of animals.

Iguanas and frogs live in forests.

Flamingos live on beaches.

Tall pine trees grow

in forests.

People in Haiti build boats

with pine tree wood.

What other things
could people in
Haiti build with pine
tree wood?

Haiti has some large cities.

Most people live in the country.

They own small farms.

They sell food at markets.

**Why might people want to go to a market to buy food?**

Every year people in Haiti celebrate Carnival.

There are parades in the streets.

People dress in costumes.

Families eat a big meal.

**What other things do you think people might do to celebrate?**

People in Haiti sometimes eat

spaghetti for breakfast.

They put hot dogs or sausage

in the spaghetti.

Soccer is a top sport

in Haiti.

Some people also

ride bikes.

People enjoy swimming too.

Haiti is a beautiful country.

There are many

things to see.

Would you like to go

to Haiti?

# Map of Haiti

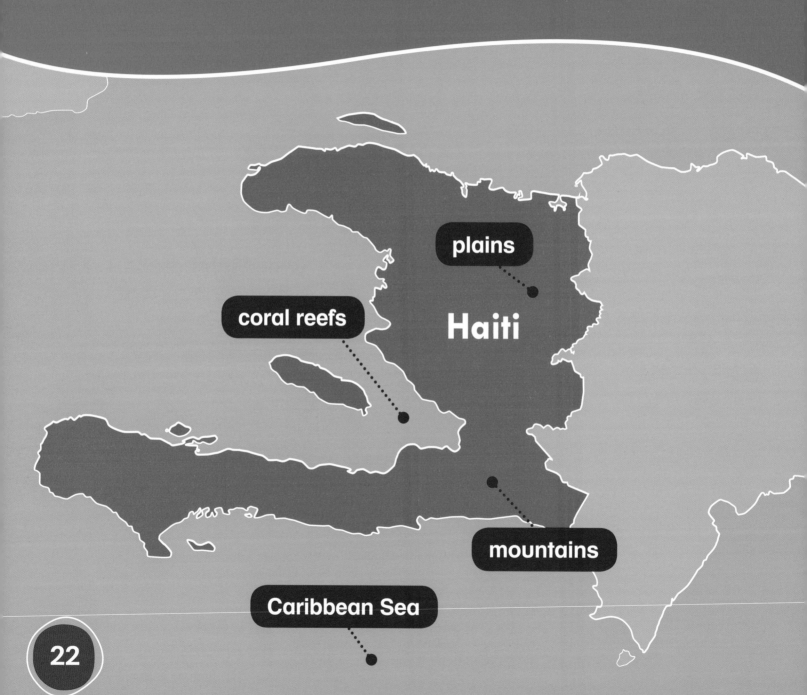

plains

coral reefs

Haiti

mountains

Caribbean Sea

# Picture Glossary

**Carnival**

a weeks-long celebration that leads up to Mardi Gras

**coral reefs**

underwater areas where many types of animals live

**island**

a piece of land surrounded by water on all sides

**plains**

big, flat pieces of land

# Read More

Kopp, Megan. *What Do You Find in a Coral Reef?* New York: Crabtree Publishing, 2016.

Parkes, Elle. *Let's Explore Australia.* Minneapolis: Lerner Publications, 2018.

Schuetz, Kari. *Life in a Coral Reef.* Minneapolis: Bellwether Media, 2016.

# Index

## Photo Credits

The images in this book are used with the permission of: © Hank Shiffman/Shutterstock.com, pp. 5, 23 (bottom left); © KSK Imaging/Shutterstock.com, pp. 6–7; © Vincent St. Thomas/Shutterstock.com, p. 9; © Suchan/Shutterstock.com, pp. 10–11; © glenda/Shutterstock.com, p. 12; © MaestroBooks/iStock.com, pp. 15, 23 (top left); © Lauri Patterson/iStock.com, p. 16; © arindambanerjee/Shutterstock.com, pp. 18–19; © Deviatov Aleksei/Shutterstock.com, pp. 20–21; © John_Walker/iStock.com, p. 23 (top right); © Kosarev Alexander/Shutterstock.com, p. 23 (bottom right).

Front Cover: © dmc5080/iStock.com.